Rebekah Huetter

In Search of My Heart

In Search of My Heart

A true, hope-filled story of one
person's heroic triumph
over the effects of childhood abuse.

Rebekah Huetter

P.O. Box 10597
Albuquerque, NM 87184-0597
www.wordsofhope.com

"First Printing" September 1997

Library of Congress Catalog Card Number: 97-60601
ISBN: 0-9658438-0-7

Dedicated first and foremost to
the millions hurt as children,
to those whose monsters were real,
those who were robbed of the joy of being a child.
May this book encourage you to heal and may
God fill you with synergism
(in the theological sense that divine grace and
human activity cooperate in the work of regeneration).

O Lord our God,
other masters besides You have ruled over us,
but we will acknowledge
and mention Your name only.

They [the former tyrant masters] are dead,
they shall not live and reappear;
they are powerless ghosts,
they shall not rise and come back.
Therefore You have visited and made an end of them,
and caused every memorial of them
[every trace of their supremacy]
to perish.

Isaiah 26: 13 and 14

Amplified Version

ACKNOWLEDGEMENTS

To my Lord and Savior, the God of Love and Life.
Thank you for showing me how you grieve
at the hurts we humans inflict on one another
and how you delight in our restoration and healing.

To my loving husband, Rick, whose love made possible
this story and whose support made possible the telling of it.

To my Mother, Sandy, who faced the ghosts of her past
and showed me by example how to heal. Her love of life
taught me how to toast the beginning of a new day
with a wine glass full of orange juice. I will
always love and admire you for your commitment
to love, truth and God.

To my four Sisters, Kathy, Rhonda, Susie, and Vickie
I love and admire each of you.

And last but not least, to my three children
Stephanie, Mike, and Eric whom I love dearly.

Special thanks to Lori Van Note for the use of her talents as
a Graphic Designer and her sweet nature.

A heartfelt thank you to Mr. Bob Bennett whose music
impacted my life causing me to embrace the healing that
the Lord intended and for allowing me to bless others with
those lyrics in this book.

PREFACE

The driving force to tell my story came to me as
my counselor proclaimed, beaming from ear to ear
like a proud parent, that I had "done it!" Instead of
feeling pleased about my accomplishment, I was
angry. For twenty-four years I had been deceived; I
had bought into the lie that I could not face the past.
But as I stood on the other side looking back on what
seemed like the Valley of Death, I saw nothing but a
smokescreen and a heroic image of myself.

For me, the journey took years and the sorrow
melted away slowly. My only hesitation in sharing
my story is knowing that there are others in this
world that have suffered worse. It is not my intention
that you feel sympathy for me, I have benefited great-
ly from my experiences on the road life led me down.
If this book causes you uneasiness then I am thankful
your soul has been stirred and your spirit awakened
to the truth about the impact of abuse on a child. The
original purpose of this book was to provide hope to
those who are forced to reconcile with a painful past,
to those that make the courageous effort to heal.
However, it is also my intention to educate the gener-
al population about child abuse, to be a voice for
those whose voices are too faint to be heard.

TABLE OF CONTENTS

INTRODUCTION

As you read this book, it is important to me that you know what kind of person I am. I'm a regular person. By "regular" I mean average, just like your neighbor next door, your good friend. You may even see some similarities between yourself and me. I have worked full-time since I was eighteen, struggling to provide for myself and Stephanie, my daughter. I was a single parent for nine years after my first marriage of eight years ended. I am not someone easily given to persuasion or wild imaginations. My family and close friends use words and phrases like "pragmatic, reality-based, truth-at-all-costs" to describe me.

In every job throughout my career, my ability to learn quickly, my dedication, and my hard work were acknowledged by my superiors with promotions and raises. While going through the experiences I have written about in this book, I held an upper management position as the Manager for the Lender/School Relations Department for the New Mexico Educational Assistance Foundation, an organization designated to oversee the federal student loan programs on a state level.

During my nine years at the Foundation, I became quite knowledgeable regarding the federal regulations governing the loan programs. Because I am so pragmatic, learning and interpreting the complicated federal regulations came easy to me. In the position I held it was necessary not only to know the current regulations but also to know the history and past regulations of the loan programs since I dealt with student loan borrowers that might have borrowed prior to the existing terms and conditions. I was respected by the Financial Aid Directors and Lenders throughout the state for my in-depth knowledge of the federal regulations.

My ability to decipher the complicated regulations and communicate this information to the Lenders and Schools that participated in the student loan programs and to the parents and student borrowers came easy to me. When my immediate supervisor recognized my talent for communicating the complicated information, she gave me the responsibility for writing and producing the publications used by lenders and schools and for the numerous brochures and information packets for student loan borrowers in New Mexico.

The Foundation was recognized at a national level for the student loan borrower counseling materials I developed. We were asked to be Presenters and provide information at a national conference in Boston Massachusetts on the entrance counseling process and materials we were using in New Mexico. I was also responsible for writing and producing a financial aid packet distributed to each high school senior throughout the state. This packet provided seniors and parents with information on the federal student aid process and programs available.

Another facet of my job was public speaking. I seemed to have a natural talent in this area, and my knowledge of the federal regulations and the federal student aid process made me confident as I spoke to audiences. The audiences ranged in size from ten or twenty to hundreds and included high school parents learning about the federal student aid process, student loan borrowers learning about the specifics of the loan programs on which they were borrowing, and Financial Aid Directors and Lenders being trained on the student loan programs they worked with on a daily basis. No matter how small or large the audience, my poise, friendly personality, and sharp wit always won their hearts. My public speaking experience led to my starring in several counseling videos for student loan borrowers and three public service commercials that informed the state's residents of the federal student aid process and programs available. In one commercial I co-starred with the governor of our state. Over the years my colleagues became more than business associates; most of them became friends.

I have given you these details of my background because it is important to me that you know I am not a person that lives in a world of fantasy but rather a person committed to reality.

I hope this book will encourage those of you that were victims of abuse to heal, to reclaim your right to happiness. For those of you whose bodies or spirits were never bruised as children, my hope is that this book will enlighten you to the impact of abuse.

Becky

CHAPTER ONE
SWIMMING UPSTREAM

It was a chilly Saturday in October of 1990. As evening approached, the curtains were drawn and darkness fell over the room. I sat on the edge of the bed thinking about my life, wondering if I would ever know what it was like to be happy. The last few years had been difficult. Most of the time I felt torn between parenting my thirteen year old daughter, Stephanie, and the demands of my job. But Stephanie was doing well, and I was at the top of my career as the Manager of Lender/School Relations Department. So why wasn't I happy?

I sat there in the darkness taking inventory of my life, trying to understand the overwhelming sadness that had always been part of my life. I realized how incredibly alone I felt. I wanted someone to spend my life with but something kept me from letting anyone close. I had met a guy in January that I knew would be good to me. Rick fit my description of someone I felt I could spend my life with, and, most important-ly, he was ready for a commitment. But after four months of dating I told him, "Find someone else. I'm not the one for you." I was baffled by my behavior. After eight years of being single I'd finally found someone that would be a good husband, someone that I was physically attracted to, and what did I do?

I ended the relationship! He was as confused by my actions as I was, but he continued to keep in touch by calling or dropping by occasionally.

The more I thought about my life, the more depressed I became. I began to cry. It seemed as if this dark cloud of sadness that hovered overhead would never leave. There was a knock at the door. It was my mother. When I opened the door she could tell that I had been crying. She asked, "What's wrong?" I sat down on the couch and answered, "I'm just depressed." She sat down beside me, put her arm around me and said, "I can see that you're depressed. Looking back, it seems like you've been this way all your life. Maybe you should see a counselor." She was right. Life had always been difficult for me. I had always felt like a fish swimming upstream, struggling against the current. The day I became aware of my struggle with life was at my great uncle's funeral. I was fifteen. I remember standing beside the coffin, thinking that just a few days before he was strong and full of life. Then suddenly, without a moment's notice, his life ended. He had fallen asleep at the wheel. His new blue Buick veered off the interstate in Southern New Mexico and he died instantly of a broken neck. I stood there looking at him, aware that his spirit was gone. His body looked like an empty shell deserted by a sea creature. I remember looking at everyone dressed in black and wondering if they were mourning, or if they were like me—envious. All I could think of as I stood there was *You lucky guy! It's over for you! No more struggling, no more stress!*

My attitude about life was a simple acceptance of life's difficulties. I never really felt sorry for myself because I thought life was difficult for everyone. I remember a friend whose baby was born with a defective heart and other major health problems. She told me of a conversation she had with the baby's doctor. He described the tremendous pain her new-born infant was suffering. She asked the doctor, "But how can she be hurting that much when she never cries?" The doctor replied, "Pain is all that she has known." As I walked away, tears filled my eyes; I understood completely the infant's tolerance of pain.

All my life I had been able to cope with the daily struggle of living by pretending I was strong, that everything was fine. For the first time in my life I was relieved that I could finally admit that I was having a difficult time. I no longer had the stamina to swim upstream; the current was too strong. My defenses were crumbling; I was no longer able to hold back the overwhelming sadness with a smile and pretend everything was okay. It wasn't.

I decided to enter counseling.

In Search of My Heart

CHAPTER TWO
THE JOURNEY BEGINS

In *Modern Man In Search of A Soul* C.G. Jung wrote;

Every one of us gladly turns away from his problems; if possible, they must not be mentioned, or, better still, their existence is denied. We wish to make our lives simple, certain and smooth—and for that reason problems are tabu. We choose to have certainties and no doubts—results and no experiments—without even seeing that certainties can arise only through doubt, and results through experiment...

When we must deal with problems we instinctively refuse to try the way that leads through darkness and obscurity. We wish to hear only of unequivocal results and completely forget that these results can only be brought about when we have ventured into and emerged again from the darkness. But to penetrate the darkness we must summon all the powers of enlightenment that consciousness can offer (pages 96 & 97).

For thirty-four years I was able to turn from my problems, to deny their existence, but the curse of consciousness had been placed on me and I could no longer pretend that life was great. I entered counseling deeply depressed. The counselor suggested that I complete a series of psychological tests. Within a few weeks the test results were in and we went over them together. He said, "The tests reveal that you are in serious denial, that you want things to look good. They also indicate that you are extremely angry." As he discussed the test results I sat there and listened. I had always considered the views and opinions of others, not that I was easily persuaded from my own opinions if I disagreed. I went home and thought about the session and the results of my tests. I remembered a dream I'd had two years before. I dreamed I was holding a young girl in my lap. It appeared that she was ten or twelve years old. She was weak and could not sit up on her own as if she had suffered early in life from a life-threatening illness. With my arms wrapped around her, I held her close, overwhelmed with the love I felt for her. She was the picture of childhood innocence. She had beautiful big brown eyes; her hair was thin, exposing her elegantly shaped head. She wore diamond-studded earrings. I sensed that this young girl could have been royalty: she had a numinous quality about her. As I held her tightly and caressed her, I sobbed until my chest hurt. I was aware that she was tied to life by a thin thread. I grieved for her frailty, knowing that each breath could be her last. I awoke from this dream sobbing deeply, my chest aching from grief. I knew she was me.

I went to my next counseling session with the realization that the condition of this little girl was directly related to the effect of my childhood abuse. After careful deliberation I knew the test results were accurate: I was angry, furious at the overwhelming destruction my father had caused in my life. I was also angry with my mother for not having done a better job of protecting me from him. All of my life I'd pretended to be strong. I had survived by denying the devastation. I knew life had always been a struggle, but I had survived. I had convinced myself that I was fine, until now. I was having to admit the truth. My childhood was a war and I was missing in action.

I was relieved that the secret was out, the secret I'd kept from myself. I didn't have to live a lie anymore. I could finally admit that I was not as strong as I had always pretended to be. Admitting my anger meant having to embrace the pain of my childhood. And that resulted in the realization that I had survived by living without feelings. I tried to explain this survival technique to my counselor in one session: "My feelings," I said, "are disconnected from me, secured at a safe distance. They're tethered safely overhead, about two feet up, like a balloon filled with helium tied to a child's wrist so that it cannot fly away."

I told of an incident. "When I was twelve, Mom and Dad were separated. Mom was working at construction sites cleaning new apartments, trying to support me and my four sisters. One day, all five of us were in the front yard playing tag, waiting for Mom to get home. Our dog Heidi, a little brown dachshund, was playing with us as if she were one of us.

As we played, running from one side of the yard to another, Heidi ran out into the street and was hit by a car. I remember the incident in slow motion. I heard the tires squeal and Heidi yelp as she was thrown to the side of the road. I ran over to her and she looked up at me with her deep brown eyes that penetrated to the very core of my being. She was as much a part of the family as my sisters and I. I ran down the street to get Buddy, our Pastor. My younger sister says he had to shoot Heidi. I don't remember that. I do remember his putting Heidi in a cardboard box, and burying her in our back yard. When Mom got home, the burial was over and Buddy was sitting on the sofa with his arms around all five of us, trying to console us in our grief. Everyone was crying except me. Rhonda, my younger sister, accused me of being cold-hearted because I was not crying like everyone else. She was right. I was cold hearted. My heart had frozen earlier in life; it stopped feeling long before Heidi's sudden death. Her death confirmed the unspoken fear that we lived with on a daily basis—our lives could come to an abrupt end just like Heidi's had."

I went on to explain to the counselor, "You see, I learned early in life the only way to survive was not to feel - it hurt too much. My heart beats, but it's only to keep my body alive; it does not feel. If I allowed myself the tears, the dam might develop a crack. My survival is dependent on not feeling." Later that evening I recorded in my journal, *"Anymore, I feel numb! I'm not happy - I'm not sad - I'm not sure I'm even alive! I think maybe I died and I never realized it and nobody else did either."*

CHAPTER THREE
REIGN OF TERROR

Embracing my childhood was difficult because most of the first twelve years of my life were blank. It troubled me that what little I could remember from my childhood were, for the most part, bad memories. I knew there had to have been more good times than I was remembering. I had childhood photographs depicting some of those times. Not being able to remember my childhood bothered me so much that at one point I sat down in the middle of my living room floor with some of the photographs, determined to force myself to remember. It was no use. The pictures left me with a keen awareness of a void, a sense that something was missing. Even though I'm in the pictures, it's as if it were someone else.

There's a picture of me on my fifth birthday, dressed in a plaid dress with my hair pulled back in a ponytail with a ribbon. My birthday cake is on a small table in front of me. Mother took the picture just as I was leaning over the cake sticking my finger into the frosting for a taste.

The next picture is of another birthday. I'm not sure if it was my seventh or eighth birthday. The glare from the sunlight makes it difficult to count the candles. In this picture three of my sisters and I (Vickie wasn't born yet) are seated on the front porch steps with me holding my birthday cake. Everyone in the picture is smiling, obviously filled with delight.

Another picture shows me jumping for joy as I look at a little Timex wristwatch, a Christmas gift. From the smile on my face, I must have wanted the watch very badly. There is no denying that the pictures are me. Why can't I remember? Except for the bad memories, it was as if I had amnesia. It felt as if someone had stolen my childhood.

Looking at the pictures reminded me of how much I love each one of my sisters and how important they have always been to me. The oldest, Kathy, has always been pretty with thick curly hair and a wonderful smile. She has loved each of her younger sisters as only an older sister can. I had a cherished photo of Kathy with her arms around me to prove the point.

I was born second in line when Kathy was two. Rhonda, was born next two years later. She's full of life and also pretty with gorgeous locks of pale blonde hair. Susannah was born forth in line when Rhonda was three. Susie has beautiful big brown eyes and dark curly hair. Victoria is the youngest. She was born when Susie was three. Vickie is the tallest of all five girls and, like the rest, is pretty with a beautiful smile.

My mother is a pretty woman with blonde hair, blue eyes and a slender frame. She is a warm, loving person. The few good childhood memories that I had were directly related to my mother's ability to love. I remember once when I was little I fell and scraped my knee. I was crying as she was doctoring my injury. When she looked up at me, I could hear the sympathy in her voice as she said, "I'm sorry." I looked at her and asked, "Why? You didn't do it." She smiled at me and finished putting the band-aid on, then hugged me and sent me on my way. She loved each of us unconditionally. I always knew that she loved me and appreciated my individuality. She tells a story about me when I was eight years old. I wanted to bake a double layer cake. She told me that two layer cakes were difficult to make, but I insisted that I could do it. Instead of discouraging me, she let me try. To this day she still says it was a delicious cake. Mother often played the piano. She also played piano in the church we attended, but Daddy hated her playing at home or in church. He hated her taking us to church. He said she was weak because she needed God.

My father was a handsome man with dark blonde curly hair, deep blue eyes, and a wide winning smile. He was warm, loving, engaging, brilliant, and fun; he was also volatile, self-centered, self-serving, and sadistic. When things were going good for Daddy, life was great for everyone. When things weren't going Daddy's way, we all suffered. Success was easy for him; with little effort he rose to the top. His employers rewarded his intelligence and ability to learn quickly with promotions and raises. Unfortunately, however, my father's dark side regularly sabotaged his good-standing, or he would get bored and come home to announce that we were moving to another city or state. Daddy was a paradox.

My Mother's parents played a significant role in my life. My grandmother was half Irish and half Cherokee. In my early years, Granny was the only role model I had of an independent woman. In her younger days, she was a real spitfire. Shortly after she married my grandfather, she returned home to visit her parents, wearing men's trousers and with her hair cropped short. She knew her parents' heads would spin because she had never been allowed to cut her hair or wear pants. From the pictures I've seen, she was a dark haired beauty with deep brown eyes and ruby red lips. She was independent and had been all her life: for example, she owned the first Merle Norman cosmetic studio in New Mexico. When my mother was a little girl, Granny and Papa owned the #9 Taxi Cab Business in Las Cruces. The phone number was also #9. For years Granny drove a taxi in a day and time when most women did not work outside the home. When I was a child Granny was a minister of the gospel. Mother said Granny had a Saul of Tarsus conversion to Christianity when she was thirty-six years old. During her ministry she did missionary work in Mexico and was instrumental in establishing several churches. Also, she traveled throughout much of the United States preaching the gospel. She could deliver one of the most effective hell, fire, and brimstone messages I've ever heard.

My grandfather was tall and lanky. In the early part of his life he was the Foreman of the Flying V

Ranch, the second largest ranch in Oklahoma during that time. When I was little he told me tales about busting broncos, riding fences, and looking for strays. Papa loved to sing old cowboy songs like Strawberry Roan and Get Along Little Doggie. You could tell by the look on his face when he sang those old cowboy songs that those were good years. During his later years he worked in the oil fields and on off-shore drilling rigs in the North Sea, the Bahama Islands, and Spain. When I was little, Papa would visit several times a year. We always looked forward to seeing him. Life was full of magic when Papa pulled up in the driveway. The first thing he did when he came to visit was to go to the grocery store and buy Oreo cookies, bananas, Cokes, and ice cream.

Sometimes Papa would visit when school was about to start, and he would take us shopping for school clothes. He would buy each of us a new dress, panties, socks, and new shoes. He used to save his pocket change in a cup on the floorboard of his car and we would live in anticipation of the moment when he would turn to one of us and say, "Go to the car and get the cup full of change." We would squeal with delight as the ceremony began. We would all run to the car and watch as the designated sister carried in the cup full of money. Then we would all five sit in a circle on the floor and divide the cup full of change: first the quarters, then the dimes, nickels and pennies.

When Papa visited, he brought us a magic kingdom. We sat around eating bowls of ice cream listening to Papa tell us tales about bathtubs full of ice cream he had at home and money trees growing in his backyard. I can remember sitting next to him at the kitchen table, early in the morning, drinking a mixture of half milk and half coffee with lots of sugar, of course. With a wink and a pat on my leg, he'd lean down close to my ear and whisper, "You know Poppie loves you." He was right, I did. Unfortunately, those moments were all too rare. When Papa left, the magic kingdom disappeared with him and we were forced to return to the existence that was more familiar to us.

Life with Daddy was filled with chaos. We were at the mercy of his moods and always uncertain of what to expect. He was a self-contained paradox: he could be a scary monster or he could be very loving. I remember one incident from my childhood that vividly illustrates both sides of his personality. When I was eleven, I was roller skating one evening after dinner. My friend was riding her bicycle and I grabbed onto the back. When she turned around in our driveway, I went flying into the grass. I fell back and tried to catch myself, but I landed on my right arm and broke it. I ran inside screaming. Mother grabbed a towel and put it around my arm. Daddy helped me to the car. I sat in the front seat between him and Mom as we drove to the hospital. I was sweating. Everything seemed kind of hazy. When we got to the emergency room they put me in a wheel-chair. I was trembling from the pain and was terri-fied. As I sat in the hallway of the emergency room shaking all over, Daddy knelt down in front of me and put his hand on my knee. He said, "Don't worry Sugar, Daddy's gonna' take care of you." His words comforted me instantly.

The doctors said it was a compound fracture and would require surgery. Because I had just eaten dinner, the doctors postponed surgery until morning. They sent me home with pain medication, a temporary cast, and explicit instructions not to eat or drink after midnight. I was to return at eight o'clock the next morning for surgery. I slept on a roll away bed in Kathy's room that night. She says I moaned all night long.

I was glad when morning finally arrived. With it came hope for relief from the tremendous pain I had endured all night. That morning as I was admitted to the hospital for surgery, I was scared. I had heard stories of people that had been put to sleep for surgery and didn't wake up. I remember lying on the operating table and questioning the anesthesiologist about his credentials.

When I woke up, I was in a hospital room with Mother standing beside my bed. The first thing I did was to look down at my arm. Seeing that I had the same kind of cast on it, my heart sank. I started crying, thinking I still had the surgery ahead of me. I had survived this trauma like all the other traumas in my life, thinking in a while it will be over and I can look back on the experience and be glad that it is in the past. When mother realized why I was crying, she explained that the cast was a different one and that the surgery really was over. Mother asked if she could stay with me that night, but the nurses explained that it was against hospital policy and she would have to go home.

Later that night, about two o'clock in the morning, I fell out of bed onto the hard, cold floor, landing on my broken arm. I stumbled to the nurses station crying, "I need my mother!" They called her. Mother came directly to the hospital and spent the rest of the night with me. The next day Daddy came to the hospital. He was angry about being awakened in the wee hours of the morning and angry that Mother had spent the night at the hospital with me. He decided that it was time for this ordeal to be over with; we were leaving. He started toward the door. Mother was trying to reason with him, "Ronald, we can't leave yet. The doctor will be in to see her soon. As soon as the doctor releases her, we'll go." But he wouldn't listen; he had made up his mind. As we made our way down the hall, the nurses were calling after him, "Sir! You can't leave, the doctor has not released her yet!" Daddy, who was never one to conform to rules or obey orders, didn't care. I remember being overwhelmed with embarrassment as I walked through the parking lot in a hospital gown and panties. I could also see the embarrassment on Mother's face. Daddy dropped me and Mother off at home, put his fishing gear in the car and left. It was obvious that his priority was fishing and not me.

I knew when we were little that Daddy hit us and I knew he could be mean. My ability to detach myself from my feelings allowed me to survive. I could recite instances of abuse very matter-of-factly, like a robot without emotions.

When I was two years old, my mother was pregnant with Rhonda. Daddy had decided that he would potty train me before the arrival of the new baby. He was going to get me up in the night to take me to the bathroom. One night he woke up too late—I had already wet the bed. Mother was awakened by my screaming and ran frantically to the bedroom. Blood was running down my face and I was crying hysterically. Daddy had slapped me for wetting my bed.

When I was little, I was always into things. I was curious by nature, and my curiosity sometimes got the best of me. Once I smeared cold cream all over my mother's dresser. Another time I tried to clean her new couch with a big bottle of Ivory dishwashing detergent. Then I ruined a huge bottle of Cheezwhiz by mixing in a can of pepper. Mother tried to protect me in my creative adventures by either cleaning up my mess or conjuring up a story so Daddy would not know what had really happened. But the time I mixed together a large bottle of ketchup and mayonnaise, he caught me red-handed. As I sat in the middle of the kitchen table mesmerized by the red and white colors swirling around and around, blending into the most beautiful shade of orange I had ever seen, Daddy walked into the kitchen and caught me. He became enraged and began to scream, "You're going to eat that entire bowl of ketchup and mayonnaise for breakfast, lunch, and dinner until it's gone!" And he saw to it that I did. Finally, a few days later, without Daddy noticing, Mother poured the remainder down the sink.

When I was seven I had long hair that Mother kept neatly pulled back into a ponytail with a ribbon. One day I was playing with my doll and decided to cut her hair. Later that evening, Daddy found my doll with the hair cropped closely to its head. Again, without prior notice, he became enraged. He grabbed a pair of scissors, yelling "I should cut off your ponytail. I should do to you what you've done to your doll." As the scene deescalated, he raised his hands, the scissors in one hand and my long ponytail in the other. Mother screamed, "Ronald!" I was left with half inch sprouts of hair at the crown of my head, graduating outward to four-and five-inch lengths. Mother says she was able to even out the layers and that it looked like I had a pixie cut which was in style back then, but she always tried to make things okay. Kathy says that as Daddy came toward me that day, I just stood there with a blank look on my face as if I were in shock.

For most children, learning to ride a bike is a fond childhood memory. For me it was just one more trauma. I learned to ride Kathy's bicycle at the age of seven, but not because I wanted to. The bicycle was big and awkward and I was afraid of falling, but Daddy insisted it was time I learned to ride. Today was the day. Terror gripped my heart as I was forced up onto what seemed like a mountain of metal. Daddy stood behind me with the back tire between his legs to steady it as I climbed on. He was holding the bicycle seat with one hand and a two-by-four in the other. I climbed up on Kathy's bicycle crying. I didn't know which to be more afraid of, the bicycle or Daddy. He was yelling "I'm going to beat you with this two-by-four if you don't ride this damn bicycle." I had learned early in life to be prepared for the worst. I rode the bike, with him running close behind, tears streaming down my face, peddling as fast as I could, wishing I could outrun him. Shortly after this incident Daddy came home and announced that we were moving to Texas.

Facing Daddy when he was angry was always overwhelming. For example, there was the time when I was eleven that I got into a normal sibling tiff with Rhonda. Daddy became angry with us and yelled, "Go to my bedroom and wait for me. I'll be in there in a few minutes to whip you!" I stood beside his bed petrified, wondering how badly we would be hit. I always knew there was the chance that he might not control himself and I could end up dead. When he finally opened the door and began the ceremony of removing his belt, I was so terrified that I lost control of my bladder and wet myself. There I stood in a puddle of my own urine.

That wasn't the only time I wet myself. As a child, life was so stressful that I wet the bed until I was twelve. I actually remember lying in bed wondering how I would explain my bed-wetting to my husband when I married! My three younger sisters also wet their beds. I had never associated bed-wetting with the daily stress until the day Mother finally told Daddy it was over. That very night all four of us quit wetting the bed!

The physical abuse was obvious: no one denied that Daddy hit us. The emotional abuse and the impact of it had to be denied for the sake of survival. I remember an incident when I was nearly twelve. It was night and the house was dark. Everyone was in bed. I needed to go to the bathroom but was afraid to go alone. I finally convinced Rhonda to go with me. Quietly, we made our way down the hall. The bathroom was only three feet from Mother and Daddy's bedroom. After using the bathroom we quietly turned off the light and began to tiptoe back down the hall to our bedroom. Suddenly Daddy's bedroom door flew open and he screamed, "YOU'RE LUCKY I DIDN'T PUT A KNIFE IN YOUR BACK . I THOUGHT YOU WERE A BURGLAR!" We let out a shriek and bolted to our bed. He laughed. I'm convinced he enjoyed his sadistic reign of terror.

Daddy had an insatiable need for control, and we were the only people in his life that had no way to escape it. When he decided to exert his control and power, like when he made me ride the bicycle and when he cut off my ponytail, there wasn't much anyone could do about it. I remember eating dinner one night and commenting that I didn't want my desert, green Jello. I disliked Jello because of the way it wiggled. I hated the taste of green Jello in particular, but Daddy decided I was going to eat it. He sat there and laughed as I ate the Jello, gagging as it came toward my mouth on the spoon.

His control was evident everywhere in our lives. He wouldn't provide Mother with money to buy groceries; then he would ridicule her saying, "My mother could make a dinner from flour and water. What's the matter with you?" There were times when the church would buy us food because Daddy would not. Mother says that when she was pregnant with Vickie, she couldn't look at women's magazines because the recipes and the colorful pictures of food made her mouth water, reminding her of how hungry she was. There was only one area of our lives that Daddy couldn't control: that was Mother taking us to church. Mother says her faith in God and His Word is what got her through those years. I believe her.

From the age of twelve I can remember my life in vivid detail as if I'd had a miraculous recovery from amnesia. The odd part of this is that Daddy's violent nature was in full force, and Mother had become the focal point of his rage. We saw her strangled, threatened with a shotgun, and thrown up against walls. One time when they were quarreling, Kathy walked out into the garage to find my father with both hands around my mother's neck. Kathy, seeing Mother's blue face, screamed and ran inside. Daddy ran in after her saying, "I'm sorry you had to see that." His apology contained no statement that he was sorry that he'd done it, just that Kathy had observed it. He offered no apology to Mom.

In the midst of this escalating violence our next-door-neighbor, Mrs. Moore, came to tell Mother she had dreamed three times that our house was covered in blood. You could hear the concern for our safety in her voice as she told Mom about her recurring dream. Mother immediately took my father's handgun to a friend's house across town. Late that evening, Judy, our pastor's wife, came over. She wanted to know how we were doing. Mom told her about our neighbor's dreams and explained that she had taken Daddy's gun to a friend's house for safe keeping because she feared that the dream might be a warning from God. Mother told Judy that Daddy's violence was at an all-time high. She listened intently to all that Mother had to say. After a few moments of silence she said, "Sandy, I think you and the girls should come home with me. Buddy needs to hear about this." Mother sat in their kitchen and repeated for the Pastor what she had told his wife. Judy and Buddy looked at each other a long time, nodding. Buddy then said, "You'd better not go back home."

Their concerns further deepened our own fears.

We found refuge that night in Granny's trailer, parked behind the church. Mother bedded us down in the dark, and we waited for sleep. Suddenly we were startled by Daddy banging on the door yelling, "Sandy, I know you're in there!" We could hear him breathing just outside the door as he rocked the trailer from side to side, ranting and raving like a madman. "Where's my damn gun? Somebody's going to die!" We all knew that we were those somebodies. I held my hand over my baby sister's mouth so she could not cry out. We had no phone, no way to call for help. No one said a word. We lay there in the darkness praying. We were victims of a war, hiding from the enemy. Eventually our enemy tired, gave up pounding on the door, and left.

Long after we left home Mother told us that she knew staying with Daddy meant certain death—it was just a matter of time. Leaving him was a calculated risk she was forced to take. She told him it was over and that he would have to leave. Surprisingly, in an effort to reconcile with Mother, Daddy, cried, joined the church, agreed to go to marriage counseling, and promised he would change. Mother had heard those same promises many times before.

The following year we continued to live in fear of Daddy's sudden appearances. He threatened, "One way or another I'll be back home." He hocked our only television set, stole our car, and burglarized our house, taking Mother's jewelry and destroying the gifts he had given her. Every time a neighbor's dog barked we were afraid it was Daddy. Even in his absence, he dominated our lives with fear. This time

Mother did not go back. The risk was too great. It was over! They divorced when I was twelve.

A year later Mother met my stepfather, Bob. He worked for the Federal Aviation Administration as an Air Traffic Control Specialist. He was a handsome man, someone that I would always love for providing me with food and a safe home for the rest of my childhood. I have always respected him for taking on the responsibility of five daughters.

With another man on the scene, Daddy slowly relinquished his control over us and absented himself from our lives. I was thirteen when he moved to Florida, we saw him twice over the next sixteen years. Even though he was gone from our lives and I was relieved that we no longer had to live in constant fear and terror, I still loved him and missed him. I wrote him letters and sent him birthday cards and Christmas cards, but they were all returned marked "Moved - Left No Forwarding Address."

In 1985, sixteen years later, Daddy called me from Florida: "Hey, Sugar, it's Daddy. Can you send me money for a bus ticket? I'm going to come and live with you girls." I was recently divorced at the time and had strong feelings about being used. I responded, "Sorry, Daddy, but I can't help you." He called Kathy and she sent him the money. When he arrived I was shocked. The years of alcohol and drug abuse had made him look old and haggard. His shoulders were slumped and his legs were thin which called attention to his stomach protruding over his jeans. His face was thin and his cheeks were sunken in from the loss of most of his teeth. His hair was gray and he had a gray beard. He was fifty-one years old and looked eighty.

He lived with Kathy while he was here. It was really hard for her. She saw Daddy's grief and wanted to make his life better, but she also understood why we felt the way we did about him. Kathy, Rhonda, and I took the opportunity to confront him about the abuse we had suffered at his hands. At the time I was aware of the physical abuse, and to some degree the terror, we lived in as children. When I asked him why he had abused us, he responded, "I did not abuse you. I never took any of you kids to the hospital with a broken bone." I said, "No. What you did was much worse. Broken bones are acknowledged with casts and medical treatment. Those injuries are obvious and cannot be denied. Memories of fear and terror are more difficult to detect, but they still impact children for life."

Kathy says that while Daddy lived with her, he marked off the days on a calendar. Each day that passed without contact with one of his daughters received a large X. She says he grieved that things were not different between him and "his girls." I wondered how he could re-enter our lives, expecting love, respect and admiration. After a year he returned to Florida.

Six months later, on Mother's Day in 1986, Daddy was killed in an automobile accident at the age of fifty-two. He was thrown from the pick-up truck he was riding in, and it rolled over on him. He died en route to the hospital with severe head injuries. His sister was notified of his death, but she refused responsibility for his burial. We were notified days later that unless we claimed his body, he would be buried by the state in a common grave. Since he was a veteran of the Korean Conflict, he was eligible for a burial plot in the Veterans' Cemetery in Santa Fe. We had his remains flown in, and he was buried without a service.

I spent several months in therapy coming to grips with Daddy's destructive force, struggling to make sense of my father's role in my life. Over the years Mother never said anything bad about Daddy. When we would begin to talk about how life was for us as children, Mother would listen. I knew it was hard for her to hear about how our childhood abuse had impacted our lives. Still she never spoke negatively about Daddy and would just sit and listen. When she did speak about Daddy, she tried to provide us with insight as to why he was the way he was. At one point, I became angry with her. I thought that I had been able to pretend my childhood was okay because she had never really talked about how incredibly mean Daddy was. Now she says, "I felt like enough damage had occurred in your lives. The least I could do was not cause any more by talking bad about your father. After all, I figured you girls could see for yourselves what he was like."

Mother had a certain sympathy for Daddy. She knew he was troubled and had a difficult childhood. In an effort to help me understand my father's abusive tendencies, Mother told me that he had been abused as a child by his mother, Mattie. Mother said Daddy told her that when he was young he would run off when his mother tried to discipline him. Late at night, he would sneak back in the house and go to bed. Many times he was then awakened in the middle of the night as his mother beat him with a piece of lumber. Like many survivors of childhood abuse, he assumed responsibility for his mother's actions. He told my mother, "I deserved it. I was a bad kid."

My mother told me about an incident where she experienced Mattie's abuse first hand. My mother was only seventeen when she and daddy were married. My father was in the Air Force. Soon after their marriage Mother became pregnant and Daddy was transferred to Newfoundland. When he left, Mother went to live with Daddy's parents back east. Early in her pregnancy Mother came down with a cold. Mattie gave her medication, insisting it would make her feel better. Within a few hours she began to cramp and soon miscarried her first child. A few days later, Mattie's sister-in-law Edith, after hearing about Mother's misfortune, came to Mother and asked. "Did Mattie give you any medication?" Mother answered, "Only for my cold. She said it would make me feel better." Edith gasped, "Mattie told me that she would see to it that you didn't have that baby back here. I'm so sorry, I should have warned you." In a state of shock, Mother phoned the doctor's office and asked the nurse about the over-the-counter cold tablets Mattie had given her. The nurse confirmed her worst fears. The tablets would definitely cause spontaneous miscarriage.

When Mother confronted Mattie, she didn't deny a thing. She sat in her chair with her legs crossed, swinging her foot from side to side, smirking, while Mother cried. Mother packed her suitcase and called her father in New Mexico, who sent her money for an airplane ticket. Before leaving, Mother told Mattie, "You will never see Ronald's children. I will see to it."

Mother claims her statement meant that she would not return with her children to visit. Mattie's husband, my grandfather, was a kind man. He had been good to my mother while she lived with them. When he took Mother to the airport, she told him what Mattie had done. She began to cry again. Filled with sadness he said, "Sandy, Mattie has used those tablets to miscarry four of her own pregnancies."

Needless to say Mattie was an incredibly evil woman. Eight weeks later, she died of a massive heart attack. My mother, little more than a child herself, had prophesied her death. Mattie never saw her son's children; Kathy, my older sister was born nine months after Mattie died. But Mattie and her evil lived on in my father.

CHAPTER FOUR
A FAILED ATTEMPT TO REWRITE THE PAST

As my feelings began to thaw and I embraced my painful past, I realized some of that pain included the dashed hopes of my marriage that had ended eight years before. My detachment from my feelings had allowed me to turn and walk away from a seven year marriage with very little difficulty. My decision to marry John had been based on the hope of rewriting my sad, unsafe childhood. I had wanted to find happiness, someone to lean on when life was difficult, and a husband that would love and care for me. John came from the kind of family I always wished I had grown up in. His father was a kind man, didn't smoke or drink, and never hit his children or wife. I knew John would never be physically abusive. I promised myself, at a very early age, that when I got married my home environment would not be a violent one. Because of my abusive past, men scared me, but John had a boyish charm that wasn't threatening to me.

When I was first dating John, my reaction to two incidents seemed very peculiar to me. The first incident happened at John's house. His twelve-year-old sister, Ashley, crawled up in her father's lap. I sat across the room watching Ashley and her father for what seemed like a very long time. The situation agitated me. Why was I so uncomfortable with Ashley sitting in her father's lap? It was obvious that there was nothing except a wholesome exchange of love between the two. I put it off to the physical abuse I had suffered at the hands of my father.

The second incident took place when John and I met his father at the airport in El Paso. At the time streaking was a fad. As we stood in the luggage area waiting for his father's luggage, three streakers ran through the terminal. What a commotion—there were gasps and shrieks as the three boys ran past, naked as jay birds. My mouth dropped open, and I stared at them in shock as they ran within several feet of me. My reaction must have embarrassed John because he jabbed me with his elbow. I gasped. I looked at him and whispered, "You have hair 'down there'?" My reaction startled me. Why did I notice the hair and not the difference in the male body? I had never seen a man naked, never looked at magazines, never been exposed to this information before in my life. I had grown up with sisters only. Why did the hair take me by surprise and not the additional body parts? This was a mystery to me.

I married John in September of 1974, after graduating from Las Cruces High School. I had just turned eighteen and he was twenty-one. John was born with severe asthma. His mother told me she used to sit up with him all night, holding him in a sitting position so he could breathe. Because of his past, John was familiar with someone taking care of him. It soon became obvious that John expected his needs to be met at all costs and that my needs were not a priority. I devoted myself to meeting John's needs—we both took very good care of him. I kept hoping things would change, that he would come to see that I too had needs. I too wanted to be cared for. But incident after incident made me know that John would not change.

One summer evening early in our marriage we drove to the neighborhood 7 to 11 to get a gallon of milk. I was not feeling well and decided to sit in the car while John went in to buy the milk. Because it was warm, the car windows were down. It was late in the evening and John had parked in the dark, on the side of the building where there was very little light. John had been in the store only a few moments when this strange looking guy came out. He walked slowly to the front of our car and stopped to light a cigarette. He had his head bowed and his hands cupped around the cigarette to block the wind while he lit it. As he inhaled his first puff from the cigarette, his eyes moved slowly up to mine as if he had been aware that I had been watching him. My heart began to pound. I knew I was not safe, the windows were all rolled down, and the doors were unlocked. I began to panic, like a rabbit caught in the headlights of an oncoming car. My heart raced with fear. There was no way I could possibly roll up the windows and lock the doors. I wondered where John was—there had been plenty of time for him to buy the milk. What was taking him so long? Suddenly, the guy pounced on the hood of our car and yelled. I jumped. At that moment John came out of the store and the strange guy turned and walked away slowly with an evil grin as if to let me know that he had enjoyed his little game. I was so relieved to finally see John. I asked, "What took so long?" He asked, "Why?" So I told him what had happened while he was in the store. John asked, "What did the guy look like?" I described him and John said, "Oh, I know exactly which guy you're talking about. I thought he might pull something like that." I screamed, "Well, why didn't you hurry then? Why didn't you come out?" He didn't answer, but I knew. John wanted someone to take care of him, not someone to take care of. I had learned that earlier in our marriage.

When I was nineteen, I found a lump in my right breast and was scheduled for surgery. For weeks I lay awake at night wondering if I would die. The surgeon assured me that at my age the lump was most likely benign, but I was still required to sign a surgical release for the removal of my breast in the event that a malignancy was found. I knew my signature on those forms meant the possibility existed that I could wake from surgery to find my breast gone and me involved in a full-fledged battle for life. The day finally arrived that I was to go to the hospital. John dropped me off at the front entrance and went back home. I was terrified as I walked through those double doors to admit myself. After filling out the necessary forms, I made my way to my room on the third floor. The phone was ringing as I walked through the door. An orderly who was making my bed stopped to answer the phone and then turned toward me to ask, "Are you Becky?" I said "Yes." He smiled and handed me the phone. My voice quivered as I said, "Hello." It was Mom. She said, "Becky, are you okay?" I started crying, "Mom, I'm really afraid." She asked, "Where's John?" I answered, "I don't know.

It's his day off, he's probably at home." Mother was furious that he had not stayed with me.

John was also impatient and intolerant when it came to my fears, and I had lots of them. One time when we were visiting his grandparents at Los Alamos, we went hiking in the Jemez mountains. John wanted to show me the natural hot springs where area residents bathed nude. On our hike we came to a shallow stream. John crossed the water without a moment's hesitation. I stood by the stream, petrified. I wanted to cross, but I couldn't make myself. He was on the other side of the stream impatiently yelling, "Come on! Cross the stupid stream!" I stood beside the stream, looking down into the crystal clear water. I could see the rocks on the bottom. The water was only ten or twelve inches deep, but it was moving fast. Why was I so terrified? It made no sense at all to me. I knew logically that the water posed no real danger, but I just couldn't get up the nerve to cross. The water was moving too fast.

As I stood there looking at the stream, I remembered a similar incident when I was about ten or eleven. I had gone on vacation with a church friend and her family. We were picnicking by a shallow stream of fast-moving water. When my friend and I walked out onto some big rocks in the stream, I slipped and fell into the water. I panicked and began kicking and splashing as if I were drowning. I felt really stupid when I finally sat up and saw that the water was only ten inches deep. My friend and her entire family were laughing at me. I was embarrassed and I remember wondering at that time too, why does this scare me?

In June of 1976 I became pregnant. I had accepted the reality that John wanted someone to take care of him and that he was not interested in returning the favor. Something strange happened during that summer, early in my pregnancy. I was lying in bed late one weekend morning, enjoying the sunshine as it streamed through the windows warming my feet. As I lay there alone, out-of-the-blue a strange thought raced through my mind. Not exactly a thought, more like a pronounced statement:

"In your womb I have planted my seed and his name shall be called Isaac."

I immediately sat up in bed. I said the words out loud then repeated them again. Was this some sort of divine prophesy? The statement was evidently an important one or it would not have come to me so distinctly. Being pregnant, my interpretation was a literal one: I was going to have a boy and I was to name him Isaac. Several months later, to my great surprise, I had a beautiful daughter. Little did I know that it would be seventeen years before I understood the meaning of those prophetic words.

Stephanie was only two weeks old when I returned to work full-time. My days began every morning at six o'clock. I would awake, get the baby fed, pack her bag for the sitter, get her dressed, dress myself, eat breakfast, load her in the car, deliver her to the sitter and then continue on to work. I was Head Teller in a bank and had to be at work by eight o'clock sharp. After working all day I would go to the sitter to pick up the baby. When I got home I would feed her, make dinner for John and myself, do dishes, bathe the baby, and get her ready for bed. By bedtime I was exhausted. Week-ends were filled with household chores, grocery shopping, laundry, mopping, and waxing floors. There was little time to relax and no time for fun.

John's daily schedule was different. He had recently taken a new job resulting in a significant increase in income. His workday began at seven in the morning and ended at three-thirty in the afternoon. By four o'clock he was relaxing on the couch, watching television, waiting for his dinner to be made.

One evening I began to talk with him about the inequality of our daily schedules. I explained how exhausted I was and that I wanted to stay home and take care of Stephanie. I suggested that his new job and increase in pay would allow me to either work part-time or quit working altogether. John's response was, "I'll divorce you if you quit!" I was crushed. I was devastated by his lack of concern for my well-being. Those six words that came out of his mouth cut deeply into my hopes and dreams of changing how life had always been for me. I realized that night that John didn't love me; he was using me to make his own life easier. I cried myself to sleep that night. The next few days I thought about my marriage. I had a mental picture of me underwater and John standing on my shoulders to keep his own head above water.

My attitude changed from innocently accepting that life is difficult to a more cynical view. I saw a bumper sticker once that summed it up for me: "Life's a bitch; then you die." I resigned myself to the fact that life would always be difficult. John was self-centered, but at least he didn't hit me.

Five years later, during a late spring afternoon nap, I had a dream. In the dream I had gotten up from my nap and was working around the house. I was doing my regular housecleaning chores when I noticed something on the bottom of my foot. I raised my foot to look and saw a thick callous peeling off; a complete imprint of my foot, like a footprint in the sand including toe prints. When I recorded this dream in my journal I wrote, the callous was off the 'soul' of my foot. A Freudian slip, I guess, because I was reaching a point in my life where I could no longer live without feeling. The "callous" was coming off of my "soul." The dream spoke a truth, a truth I needed to hear.

The dream gave me hope and made me aware of my overwhelming feelings of unhappiness. In April of 1982 after seven years of marriage, I told John I needed some space, some time alone. I was not only terribly unhappy, I was extremely angry. I was angry at John for using me throughout our marriage, and I was angry at myself for letting him.

After we were separated, I approached John once again about the inequality of our relationship. I told him, "I'm tired of giving and getting nothing in return." He responded, "Okay! Okay! I'll try to give, but I hope the pendulum doesn't swing so far in the other direction that I'm giving everything and you're giving nothing." I knew as soon as those words left his mouth that it was hopeless. Our relationship would never be give and take.

During our marriage my mother-in-law often told me, "You're the best thing that's ever happened to

John," and she was absolutely right. I took good care of him and always made sure his needs and desires were met, even at my own expense. During our entire marriage I carried the responsibility for paying the bills, childrearing, housekeeping and working full-time. I walked away from my marriage feeling like the Grand Canyon, gutted from giving. I spent almost eight years making John's life comfortable with little thought of my own needs. I had given myself away. I left the marriage knowing that life would be easier without him. As I was leaving he looked at me and said, "You'll never make it on your own." I knew he was talking about himself. He was the one that needed someone to take care of him. I needed to learn how to take care of myself.

CHAPTER FIVE
ON MY OWN

The divorce was final three weeks before our eighth wedding anniversary. Indeed, life was easier with only Stephanie, who was five at the time, to care for. I embarked on my search for happiness alone. I never liked having to depend on anyone other than myself anyway; I had learned if you depend on others, they'll let you down. I began to concentrate on myself and do special things that I enjoyed. On evenings when Stephanie was with her father, I stopped after work to pick up Chinese take-out. I'd go home, take a hot bubble bath and watch T.V. while I ate my Chinese food alone. Life was proving to be pretty good.

Mother understood why I left my marriage. She saw me give unconditionally and knew that John was self-centered and uncaring. I remember one Valentine's day when she asked, "What did you get for Valentine's Day?" I told her, "Nothing, this Valentine's Day was no different than the others, Mom. I didn't get a card or flowers." She shook her head and muttered something about John's unthoughtfulness. As much as Mother loved John, she had great difficulty with his lack of   appreciation for me. Being single meant I could dedicate myself to making sure my own needs were met.

Every aspect of my life began to reflect what I was feeling inside; I was needing some major changes in my life. I had worked at a bank for five years. As head teller of the main bank, I supervised a teller line with ten tellers, trained new tellers and balanced a vault that sometimes had more than a million dollars in it. About a year before John and I divorced, I left the bank because of stress and low pay. I went to work on a loading dock as a billing clerk making more money than I had at the bank.

Growing up I had always been the "good kid." I never experienced the normal adolescent rebellion that most teenagers go through. After my divorce at the age of twenty-five, I found myself doing things I had never done before. I had my first beer and tried to smoke my first cigarette. I found myself attracted to bikers, the tough guys with long hair, beards, tattoos, and black leather jackets. These tough guys were, for the most part, like me. They appeared tough on the outside, with their don't-mess-with-me attitudes, but once you got past their tough exteriors they were really very vulnerable.

Mother must have wondered what was going on, but she never questioned me. She was always supportive. For my twenty-sixth birthday she wrote me a poem:

Happy Birthday 26!

Tell me now Becky,
      standing on top
just how'd you pull off
      this coup 'de tat?
You with your effortless grin
      and good cheer
you who refused
      any failure by fear.
Always a winner,
      always "I can!"
never could hear any
      "no Bec, you can't."
A medal of honor,
      you'd believe that?
No! not for you Love -
      but one big black hat!

           Mom

    The first couple of years after my divorce I dated Brian. Brian and I worked together on the loading dock. He had long brown hair and a beard. He was one of those tough guys, but what really attracted me to Brian was his soft heart. One day we were talking about some vacation time I had arranged to take. Brian asked, "So, where are you going on this fun vacation you have planned?" I explained, "My mother is in the hospital in Albuquerque, and, as much as I need a fun trip, this is not it." I finished explaining how important my mother had been to me and how afraid I was to see her not doing well, he looked at me sympathetically and said, "That must be hard for you." I nodded yes, it was hard for me. That was the first time in my life a guy had shown me any sympathy. I dated Brian for two years. He was kind and thoughtful, always giving me flowers or gifts on my birthday, Valentine's day and Christmas. But we didn't have the same goals in life, and Brian had difficulty with children, so our relationship ended with me feeling pretty comfortable being single.

I had come to enjoy my independence and loved my life of solitude. I liked having my life organized and being in control. I liked doing things when I wanted to and not having to consider a partner's needs before my own. Since my divorce I had recorded my thoughts and dreams in a journal, one of my favorite pastimes. Feelings were something foreign to me; recording my thoughts and feelings helped me to understand them better, bringing them a little closer.

The next few years I concentrated on my career and raising Stephanie, occasionally meeting men and always on guard against unsuitable guys with problems. My past had taught me to stay away from self-centered men. Dating became an education process where I learned to voice my needs in relationships with the expectation of having them met. I'll never forget leaving the Sunset Bar and Grill after telling one suitor, "I'm looking for someone that wants a full-time relationship, not someone to occasionally date". In response, he told me, "I'm sorry, I'm just not at that place in my life. I want someone to have some fun with, not a serious relationship." I got up and walked away, feeling good about voicing my need and being determined that my needs would be met in a relationship or I wouldn't stay in it.

CHAPTER SIX
THE FORTRESS BECOMES A PRISON

I became expert at detecting character flaws in the men I met. Unfortunately, I also became an expert at terminating relationships. It was after saying good-bye to Stan that I began to suspect that I might have a problem. Stan was a kind person. He seemed moral, decent, responsible, and loving. I'm quite sure he would have been a good husband. We stopped dating after I told him I was not ready for a serious relationship.

It was after meeting Rick that I had to admit that I definitely had a problem. Rick loved cars and football. He didn't smoke, didn't do drugs, and he drank only occasionally. He was everything I had looked for in a guy. As strange as it may seem, Rick had many of my father's good traits. He had the natural talent of an engineer and was even employed in the same field as my father. But there the comparison with Daddy ended because Rick was a consistently warm and loving person and a good father. He had two boys named Mike and Eric from his previous marriage. He even had a bit of the tough-guy, sporting a tattoo on his left forearm. His brown, layered, collar-length hair and beard clinched the attraction for me. Within a month of our meeting, Rick pledged his commitment to me. I was fine with this until sometime later when he mentioned marriage. I could not understand my reluctance to continue seeing him, but, nevertheless, I ran.

It had been months since I said good-by to Rick, but he continued to stop by or call, always saying, "I just wanted to see how you're doing." Every time I saw him I was reminded of what a caring person he was. The life of solitude that I once cherished began to feel lonely. I began to resent my isolated existence that once felt so safe. One day I was driving down the road listening to the radio when a song titled Lord Of The Past began to play. The words caught my attention:

Every harsh word spoken, every promise ever broken
    to me, total recall of data in the memory.
Every tear that has washed my face, every moment of
    disgrace that I have known, every time I've
    ever felt alone—

Lord of the here and now, Lord of the come what may,
    I want to believe somehow that you can heal
    these wounds of yesterday.
So now I'm asking you to do what you want to do. Be
    the Lord of the past. Oh how I want you to be
    the Lord of the past.

All the chances I let slip by, all the dreams that I let die
    in vain afraid of failure and afraid of pain.
Every tear that has washed my face, every moment of
    disgrace that I have known, every time I've
    ever felt alone—

Lord of the here and now, Lord of the come what may,
    I want to believe somehow you can redeem
    these things so far away.
So now I'm asking you to do what you want to do
    Be the Lord of my past. Oh how I want you to
    be the Lord of the past

Well I picked up all these pieces and I built a strong
    deception, and I locked myself inside of it
    for my own protection.
And I sit alone inside myself and curse my company,
    for this thing that has kept me alive for so long
    is now killing me.

As sure as the sun rose this morning, the man in the
    moon hides his face tonight. I lay myself down
    on my bed, and I pray this prayer inside my
    head.

Lord of the here and now, Lord of the come what may,
    I want to believe somehow you can redeem
    these things so far away.
So now I'm asking you to do what you want to do.
    Be the Lord of my past. Oh how I want you to
    be the Lord of the past.
Words & Music by Bob Bennett ©1989 Matters Of the Heart Music

The DJ said the song was by Bob Bennett. I drove
to the store and purchased the cassette. I played the
song over and over, amazed that the words mirrored
exactly how I felt. It was true: I had learned to func-
tion so well alone. I had learned early in life that
when people get close to you they hurt you. I had
picked up all the pieces and built a strong deception,

just like the song said. I had deceived even myself that I had survived my childhood war with minimal damage. For nine years I had been single, living alone behind a locked apartment door. At one time the solitude seemed safe, like a fortress that provided protection, but then I began to feel very alone. The fortress, instead of protecting me, was beginning to feel like a prison that held me captive. As I sat and listened to the song, I began to cry. The words were speaking such truth: And I sit alone inside myself and curse my company, for this thing that has kept me alive for so long is now killing me.

In December Rick came by in his jeep and asked me to go for a drive in the snow. We drove up the backside of the Sandia Mountains to a little coffee shop that sits on the Crest. We sat by the window so we could look down on the city below and ordered hot chocolate. As we sipped our hot chocolate, Rick began to talk. "Remember how you told me you were not the one for me and that I should find someone else?" He paused to sip, "Well, I met another girl." My heart sank as he continued, "She's nice, and I like her." Then he looked up at me and said, "But you're the one I love. You're the one I want to spend the rest of my life with." I sat in silence with my head down, my eyes filling with tears. He reached across the table and took my hand in his. "Bec, whatever it is that you're going through...I'll wait, and when you've worked it through, I'll be here."

CHAPTER SEVEN
ESCAPING THE WEB OF LONELINESS

After a few months of counseling, it became obvious to me that I had difficulty with intimate relationships. Rick's promise to wait gave me renewed courage and made me determined to work out my past. Rick even attended a couple of counseling sessions with me because I so mistrusted my own judgment of men. My difficulty in accepting the possibility of a relationship with Rick led my counselor to suspect there was more than just physical abuse in my past. He said I had many of the symptoms exhibited by survivors of sexual abuse. I understood the process of diagnosing illnesses from symptoms, having worked at one time in a doctor's office. It made perfect sense that if science could be driven to heal physical ailments through the diagnosis of illnesses from a physician examining the patient's symptoms and arriving at a treatment, why would the psychological aspect of our being be any different?

In one session we discussed the impact sexual abuse has on an individual and the therapist candidly asked, "Becky, did your father incest you?" I told him: "When I was a child, I was molested, but not by my father. When Kathy was five and I was three, a woman from our church took me and Kathy home with her on Sunday afternoons. She told Mother she enjoyed our coming over to play with her children. The real reason she took us to her home was for her husband to sexually abuse us in the shed in their backyard. The "church-going" woman would bring her husband iced tea to the shed as he had his way with his prey.

It happened more than once, but one Sunday when Mother picked us up she noticed the man holding me in a peculiar way, his hand under my bottom. She grabbed me away from him. Later that day, as we ate dinner, Mother questioned me about the man and I blurted out, "He plays with bottoms." We never went to their house again.

With this revelation my counselor suggested I join a group for victims of sexual abuse. Knowing that I had been sexually abused as a small child and determined to free myself from the web of loneliness, I decided being part of such a group couldn't hurt. I agreed to join. The group was made up of five young women and a counselor, who kept the focus of the group pointed toward recovery. Details about the incidents of abuse were discouraged, but we were encouraged to talk openly about the impact of the sexual abuse in our lives. Each participant remembered the violations committed against her in vivid detail, and each one was acutely aware of the devastation suffered as a result of those violations. Throughout the eight weeks of therapy I had difficulty. My inability to feel was as much a handicap as my inability to remember my childhood. In one session, I explained to the group how my past had impacted my life: "In order to survive, I couldn't feel. It hurt too much. I have very little memory before the age of twelve. It's as if someone stole my childhood." One young woman responded, "I wish I could forget! I remember every incident with vivid details".

After having spent eight weeks with four women so obviously affected by the abuse in their past, I had to admit to myself that I must be minimizing the impact of my own sexual abuse. The group ended with the emphasis being placed on each participant taking responsibility for the role she played in the incidents of abuse. I could not understand. How could I, as a three-year-old, be responsible for what had been done to me? I certainly was not going to take responsibility for anyone who had destroyed my Garden of Eden. Whoever took away my innocence as a child, whoever defiled my Garden of Eden with sin, would have to take full responsibility because I was certain I had done nothing wrong. When the group ended, I left counseling. I needed a break.

Feeling good about the progress I had made, I finally consented to marry Rick. We were married two months later in a small wedding with family and close friends. My counselor was also an ordained minister, and we counted it an honor that he consented to perform our wedding ceremony. After the wedding we had dinner with those attending. Later that evening we had a large reception in a beautifully decorated room, celebrating with our families and many friends. Most everyone stayed and danced until two in the morning. I was celebrating more than just finding a good husband; I was celebrating freedom. I had freed myself from the web of loneliness, escaped from the prison of solitude that held me captive.

CHAPTER EIGHT
ENTERING THE VALLEY OF DEATH

Several months later I started having nightmares: dreams of men violating children, dreams of fast-moving muddy rivers, recurring dreams where I was unable to scream for help as three dogs were attacking me. I would wake from these dreams sweating, my heart pounding. Every nightmare would make me withdraw from my new husband, wishing I was alone again, safe behind a locked door. Every dream made me know how deeply I had been affected by the sexual abuse in my past. The dreams continued relentlessly, each one making me realize why I had forgotten so much of my past. I began to suspect that I had suffered more at the hands of my father than just physical and emotional abuse. In my journal I recorded, *"I am afraid to open this door. It's been nailed shut so long cobwebs have grown on it. It's a cellar door I didn't even know existed a few months ago."*

I began to hate being physically intimate with Rick. Occasionally strange physical sensations would come over me while we were making love, and I would be plunged back mentally to being an infant or young child. One time when we were making love, suddenly it was as if I were a baby and Rick was someone else, an adult male over me. I reacted instantly by pushing Rick off me and rolling over on my side, curled up in a fetal position. Every time one of these weird physical sensations occurred I knew it had nothing to do with what was going on at the moment, but still our passionate interlude would come to an abrupt halt with me in a fetal position, crying. At first, Rick worried that he had hurt me causing me to cry, but he soon came to understand that the sensations I was experiencing were the ghosts of yesterday's pains. He was always compassionate, putting his arms around me while I lay there crying. Every ghostly memory made me know exactly why I had forgotten so much of my past. It wasn't long until I began to dread the dark.

The next few months were hell. At night, I was haunted relentlessly by dreams, and ghosts from the past haunted my days. I noticed little girls everywhere. I saw them at the grocery store, at the neighborhood convenience store where I filled my car with gas, even at the hamburger stand. Anytime I saw a man with a little girl, I wondered if she was safe. I would think about how vulnerable and unprotected children are. In my journal I wrote, *"Incest is a diabolically evil sin intended to destroy the very heart of a child. It robs the victim of the ability to trust and love."*

Seeking relief from the torment, I began undergoing counseling once again in the summer of 1991, this time with a different counselor. A co-worker recommended a counselor she knew named Dick Hiester. I made the appointment reluctantly, knowing he was a man. He was soft spoken, a small man, who wore glasses and had a scholarly air about him. During the first session I told Dick about my dreams. I admitted for the first time the truth that my dreams had revealed, that I suspected my father had incested me. I was furious that I had lived my life handicapped because of his abuse: physical, mental, and now, sexual. I had been forced to live apart from my feelings, disconnected from my body. In my journal I wrote:

My life was segmented
> *shortly after birth.*
My head became residing judge,
> *memories to keep earthed.*
My feelings tethered closely by
> *so as not to lose,*
the part of me that felt the pain,
> *my heart I could not choose.*

If I had drawn a picture of me, it would have been a huge head and a tiny body. I told Dick, "My heart beats, but only to keep my body alive. I can't feel anything. I don't need alcohol or drugs to anesthetize the pain, I'm already numb. I've lived my entire life with my feelings amputated." I was angry at the devastation dealt me as a child: the physical abuse we suffered; the terror that we went to sleep with every night and woke up with every morning, never knowing when we were going to be slapped for something that was okay yesterday; the moving from town to town on a moment's notice; and—finally what was now appearing to be all too true—the traumatizing acts of incest! I knew I was going to have to face these ghosts head on. The curse of consciousness had been placed on me, and I was driven to know exactly what had happened to me as a child.

In one counseling session, as I was trying to make sense of my past and my father's impact on my life, I kept saying, "My father was evil." After I repeated the statement very matter-of-factly throughout the session, Dick asked, "Have you read Scott Peck's book People of the Lie?" I answered, "No." He walked over to the bookshelves and pulled it out. As he handed the book to me he said, "Maybe this will help you understand." The book was about human evil, and in it Dr. Scott M. Peck states

> The most typical victim of evil is a child. This is to be expected, because children are not only the weakest and most vulnerable members of our society but also because parents wield a power over the lives of their children that is absolute (page 107).

As I looked back at the impact of my father's evil force in my life, I needed to know exactly what he had done to me. I felt like this was the only way to be free from his reign. I wanted to reclaim my life, my right to happiness.

Dick and I began working back to my childhood. My memory began to return little by little. I felt like someone recovering from amnesia, one memory leading to another. I was excited to remember houses that we had lived in and memories of my mother playing Chopin's "Valis" on the piano while we girls pretended to be ballerinas on stage and danced around the living room on tip toes. I was amazed at what I was beginning to remember.

I left one session in the heat of the day. As I walked to my car a gust of wind blew a light mist from the nearby sprinklers on me. I gasped at first, shocked by the cold mist. Then as the hot air quickly warmed my skin, I smiled, remembering how much fun we had as children playing in the sprinklers on hot summer afternoons. It was an instant of welcomed relief from the tremendous pain that I was in.

As my past continued to surface, one house in particular was mysterious to me, the house on Mockingbird Lane. I could remember only bad things about that house. That was the house where Daddy made me ride Kathy's bicycle. We lived there when Daddy cut off my ponytail. The house on Mockingbird Lane was where Kathy was almost kidnapped walking home from school. I could distinctly remember the floor plan of that house. I could close my eyes and picture myself as a little girl in a tee shirt and panties standing in the kitchen and then in the living room. But I could not make myself go past my bedroom doorway, the bedroom I shared with Rhonda and Kathy. Why? I went home from the counseling session with a mental picture of myself as a little girl, standing in the doorway of that bedroom.

Even in counseling I had not dared tell about the ominous appearance of a figure in a hooded robe. He came to me occasionally as I drifted off to sleep. He moved fluidly across the room from the doorway to stand beside my bed. He looked at me saying nothing. I would be frozen with fear, unable to speak. This had happened several times over the last two years, and each time he appeared I would be instantly jolted back to consciousness, left with an overwhelming sense of powerlessness. Late that night, as I drifted off to sleep, the man in the hooded robe came beside my bed once again. This time I spoke to him, and instantly he vanished! I couldn't believe it. For the first time I wasn't powerless to speak out against him.

During my next session, I hesitantly told Dick about the apparition that visited me. I was afraid he would think I had gone over the edge—even I was beginning to wonder. Dick sat up in his chair and took a deep breath. He asked me to tell him more about the man in the hooded robe. I knew it was unbelievable, but I explained it to him anyway: "I've seen him about eight times over the last two years. He comes as I am falling asleep. He always appears in my bedroom doorway and moves fluidly across my bedroom to stand beside my bed for only a few moments, and then he just kind of fades away. His visits always left me with an overwhelming sense of powerlessness because I was never able to speak. I would just lie there terrified. But last night was different. For the first time I was able to speak as he stood beside my bed, looking down at me, and he instantly vanished!" Dick asked, "What did you say to him?" I sat there for a moment thinking and then said, "I don't know exactly, but whatever it was, it worked."

I sat in silence thinking about a visit Daddy had made when John and I were married. I remembered him talking about white magic and spells. I thought for a few moments about his insatiable quest for control and power over us as children. I looked at Dick and said, "You know, my father was always drawn toward the dark side of life."

I had always prided myself on being honest. I had been raised to live by God's Laws, one of which is— "Thou shalt not lie." My personality type did not lend itself to imaginations. I was pragmatic and reality based. This was all getting pretty weird, and I knew my family was never going to buy what was surfacing; yet in my heart I knew I was not imagining these things.

I finally got up the nerve to ask Mother about the house on Mockingbird Lane and the bedroom where I'd slept. I asked her to tell me all she knew about that house. She thought for a few minutes and then said, "I hated that house. I never wanted to move into it." She sat there with a somber look on her face. "That house had human feces smeared on the walls before we moved in. That was one of the rare times that I ever withstood your father. I remember telling him, "There is no way I am moving into that house." Your father was so intent on living there that he actually cleaned the house himself. He was determined to have his way." I asked Mother, "Mom, what about the lady that owned the house?" Mother said, "She was kind of strange. She always dressed in black and went to Mass every day. I remember that she had a child who died young. She sat a place for the little girl at dinner every night."

One of my dreams involved three women chanting in a dark room with candles lit. I knew one of the ladies in my dream was the landlady that owned the house on Mockingbird Lane. I could even remember her name.

In Search of My Heart

CHAPTER NINE
THE PUZZLE TAKES SHAPE

While trying to unravel the mystery of my past, work was getting more and more difficult. During the day I was deciphering complicated federal regulations, and at night I was being visited by an apparition. I thought I was going crazy. It felt like my world was crumbling. I felt like Humpty Dumpty in pieces and all apart, but I was determined to put him back together again. Dick and I were going to do better than all the king's horses and all the king's men. I had to believe that. Dick suggested that I draw, paint, write, do anything that would help to exorcise these ghosts from my past.

One night I was finding it difficult to sleep. I got up and went into the guest room. As I lay on the bed, I began to sweat profusely. My senses became heightened. I jumped at every creak and groan in the house. I was terrified, as if I were in the jungles of Vietnam waiting for the enemy to attack. I knew I was re-experiencing my past, a day in the life of my childhood. I never knew when the enemy would strike. He always attacked when I least expected it, like when he cut off my ponytail or when he slapped me in the middle of the night. I would be playing quietly, minding my own business, and suddenly— BOOM! He'd fly into a rage, yelling and screaming.

After my experience that night waiting for the enemy, I became aware that I suffered from Post Traumatic Stress Disorder. I understood why loud, unexpected noises unnerved me so. I understood why I hated the fourth of July. I came to understand why I get so upset when someone hides around a corner and jumps out at me. These playful acts startle me to the point of rage, and then I feel badly that I cannot take a joke. I learned early in life that light-hearted play sometimes brings on unexpected attacks.

After the night I spent waiting for the enemy, I drew a picture of me as a child, playing innocently. The enemy was in the foreground waiting to attack, peering through bushes, watching me play on the rug in the middle of the living room floor.

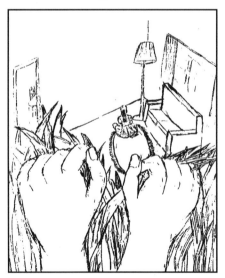

The night I spent waiting for the enemy impacted me so much that I began to wonder if I could survive any more realizations. I was beginning to appreciate my amnesia and wished I could turn back, and yet the haunting dreams continued. I told Dick, "I can't take this much longer. I have to face these ghosts. If I don't, they're going to haunt me forever." We scheduled a long session for my next appointment.

I went into that session scared of what I would leave knowing. As I entered the room that day, I remembered a verse from the Twenty-Third Psalm. I thought about how scared David must have been when he wrote, Yea, though I walk through the valley of the shadow of death, I will fear no evil for Thou art with me. At this point I could only hope that He was with me too.

I sat down on the couch terrified. Dick sat across the room in a chair. After a few minutes of silence, he asked me to close my eyes and visualize myself as a child. It took a few moments for me to relax; then a visual image appeared. Within a few minutes I began to breath shallowly. He asked, "Rebekah, how old are you?" I answered, "I'm seven." Then he asked, "Where are you?" and I replied, "I'm in the house on Mockingbird Lane. I hate this house." As the memory unfolded and I realized why, I began to cry. "I'm lying on a table in the basement." In between sobs I explained, "Daddy's dedicating me to evil. There are three women watching while he violates me." Dick asked, "What are you doing? Are you struggling or fighting?" With my head held down, in between sobs, I replied, "No. I'm just lying there." I cried for a long time. Dick sat in silence until my sobbing subsided.

I was sitting there on the couch, grieving over the evil that had been so prevalent in my childhood, when another memory began to unfold. The look on my face must have alerted Dick that I was remembering something else. He asked in a calm voice, "Rebekah, are you all right?" I answered, "Yes, I'm sitting on the rug in the living room playing with my toy monkey. Granny gave him to me for Christmas. I love him. He has long legs and arms that are black and his body is yellow. He has a soft rubber face and hands. I really love him a lot." Then Dick asked, "How old are you?" I said, "I'm five." Suddenly the pleasant memories came to a screeching halt and I stopped talking. Dick asked, "What's wrong?" I began to cry uncontrollably. I explained between sobs: "Daddy came into the room and saw me playing with my monkey. He grabbed him away from me and tore off his arms and legs. I screamed. He threw him in the trash and then sent me to bed for crying." I sat there sobbing. "How could someone be so mean?" I asked.

Dick replied, "Now I understand why you didn't fight when he was dedicating you to evil. He was a big monster for a little girl to fight." After a while, I calmed down and once again my past began unfolding in my mind, like an old family movie.

This time I was still younger. I told Dick, "Now I'm at the river in Las Cruces." "How old are you?" he asked. "I'm three. Daddy and I are at the river. We're in the car. He's in the front seat with the car door open. He's holding me in his lap." Suddenly I stopped talking, my face grimaced with pain. Dick asked, "What's wrong?" I began to cry hysterically, sobbing, "It hurts. It hurts." I cried and cried, explaining to Dick, "Daddy had me in his lap and my panties were off. He was moving me up and down on him."

It took a long time before I finally calmed down. The look on my face must have told Dick the memory was not over. He asked, "What's happening now?" I said, "He sat me down in the dirt. He's zipping up his pants. My bottom is covered with dirt and yuck." Then I got quiet again as the memory continued to unfold. "He's taking me over to the river; he's going to wash off my bottom." I began to whimper, "He knows I'm afraid of the water. He's holding me by one arm, dangling me over the water, laughing as I squirm."

We sat there for a long time with me hugging a pillow and crying. I wondered how someone could commit such diabolically evil acts against an innocent child. It took a long time for me to calm down. Once I did, Dick said, "That's enough." I agreed. I was physically exhausted and my head felt as if it were reeling from the surfaced memories. I have never been the type of person to come up with wild imaginations and certainly am not the sort of person that enjoys fantasy. I have always prided myself on being a person of truth. The last thing I wanted to do was go around telling lies about some wild imaginations. After I left the counseling session, I sat in my car for awhile thinking about what I had just experienced, about how, in my mind, it was like watching an old family movie. I was intrigued how each scene had unfolded in my mind as I watched, uncertain of what was to come next. I knew the ghosts that I had allowed to come forth were not mere imaginations.

It was weeks before I could bring myself to question Mother, but I finally got up the nerve to ask, "Mom, did I have a favorite stuffed animal when I was little?" Mother said, "Yes. Of course you did. It was a monkey Granny gave you for Christmas." I sat there for awhile thinking about the monkey with the long spindly legs and arms that had surfaced in my memory. I asked, "What happened to it?" She replied, "Oh Becky, don't you remember what your father did to your monkey?" I looked at her and answered, half hoping I was wrong, "He tore it up?" With her eyes full of sadness, she nodded her head yes. I started to cry. I was relieved, but I was also filled with sadness.

I had to know if the rest of the memories were true also. "What about when I was three. Did Daddy ever take me to the river?" Mother said "Becky, when you were little, we had picnics at the river. Don't you remember? We even had an Easter Egg Hunt there once. The river was your father's favorite place. He loved to fish." I could tell that she was remembering good times, but I was growing impatient. "Mom, when I was three, did Daddy ever take me to the river alone?" She thought for a few moments, then answered: "Well, it's possible that he did. When you were three your father was out of work for awhile and he babysat you and Kathy during the day while I worked. At that time Kathy would have been in school. Yes, I guess your father could have taken you to the river alone when Kathy was in school. Why?" I couldn't bring myself to tell her.

I was relieved that Mother was able to validate my unearthed memories. I continued with the mysterious house from my past. "Mom, remember the house on Mockingbird Lane? Was there a basement in that house?" She said, "No. It had a cellar." I was stumped. The house remained a mystery until the following week when I was reading back through my journals and read an entry I had written two years before! *"I am afraid to open the **cellar** door that's been nailed shut all my life."* That was it! Mother said the house on Mockingbird Lane didn't have a basement. It had a cellar! Coincidence? I wasn't convinced that it was.

The more I thought about the surfaced memories, the more my life began to make sense, like puzzle pieces fitting together. If the memory at the river were true, it would certainly explain my reaction to Ashley, John's youngest sister, sitting in her father's lap, and my response to the streakers at the airport. It was all beginning to make sense. That's why I wasn't freaked out about the streakers' anatomy, but was by the fact that they had hair "down there." Because Daddy had kept his unzipped pants on, I did not see any pubic hair. It also explained why I never had a natural curiosity about boys, especially since I grew up in a family of all girls. And for once in my life, I could understand my phobia of fast-moving water. These realizations made the rest of my life make sense—the missing puzzle pieces completed the picture.

The next few sessions I spent coming to grips with the raw truth. My father had indeed done evil things to me as a child. Dick started talking about wrapping up therapy, but I felt like I needed to do something in response to Daddy's evil.

I went home and thought about the fear and terror that I lived in as a child, how I'd wet the bed for twelve years because of Daddy's reign of terror, how I stood beside his bed waiting for him to whip me and wet myself like an animal when he appeared in the doorway. I wanted him to know how humiliated I had been. I thought about the evil choices he had made in his life, how he loved control and power, and how he so delighted in his reign of terror.

With Rick's help, I devised a plan, a symbolic act of retaliation against my father's evil. It took me a week, but I finally found a life-size greenware skull at a local ceramic store. It was perfect. The next step was to plan a trip to Daddy's grave. The morning arrived that I would confront my father's evil. I got dressed, ate breakfast, and before leaving the house urinated in a jar. With the lid on tight, I put the jar and the skull in a paper sack and drove to Daddy's grave in Santa Fe. I sat there for a long time thinking about my life, wishing things could have been different. I cried over my losses, wishing I'd had a father whose lap was safe, wishing I'd had a father who protected his children instead of terrorizing them.

I took out the jar of urine, removed the lid and poured it on his head stone. I said: "How does it feel? I remember the day you sent me and Rhonda to your room. I remember how scared I was when you appeared in the doorway and took off your belt to whip us. I was humiliated as I stood beside your bed with pee running down my legs, standing in a puddle of urine. I also remember how humiliated I was that I wet the bed until I was twelve because of the fear you caused in my life. Why were you so mean? Were you trying to make us mean? I know your mother was mean to you, but you could have chosen to be good to your children."

As I sat there thinking about his life, I knew he had never taken responsibility for his choices. I continued my speech: "Daddy, I believe that inside each of us we have the potential for both good and evil. You never took responsibility for your choices in life. Just because you refused to hold your mother accountable for the abuse she inflicted on you as a child, doesn't mean that we shouldn't hold you accountable. Ultimately, we're all responsible for the choices we make. I believe you came to many crossroads in your lifetime. Your choices led you down the path you took."

As I sat there thinking about Daddy, I knew he wasn't always evil. I knew it was his predilection, his preference, his choice of wrong, evil, bad—whatever you want to call it. Those choices he made over the course of his life, caused him to actually become what he consistently chose.

My last statement that day at the grave was a proclamation to reclaim my life, my right to happiness. Standing beside his grave I said, "Your abuse and terror severely affected the first twelve years of my life. There wasn't a lot I could do about it; I was a casualty of the war. The next twenty-four years of my life I lived in reaction to those years of abuse and terror suffered at your hands. But now I'm thirty-six years old, and I am tired of living in reaction to the evil you inflicted on me as a child. I'm taking back my life. I'm going to learn to be happy somehow." Then I took the skull and in a ceremonial act raised it to the sky and crushed it on his head stone. I continued my proclamation: "In retaliation to your evil choices that have impacted my life, this skull is symbolic of your love of evil. The broken pieces symbolize the impact you had over me. As the rain dissolves these pieces, so will your evil influence over my life dissolve."

CHAPTER TEN
IN SEARCH OF MY HEART

The next counseling session I told Dick about my visit to Daddy's grave. I was beginning to understand why I saw life so black and white, wrong and right. Mother told me there were times in life when situations presented a gray area, but I never saw it. I started to understand that this black or white view of life was a result of my childhood experience of living with my father and my mother. I saw that struggle on a daily basis between my parents: Daddy as bad, and Mother as good. There you have it—Satan and God under the same roof, married. I began to see why I was aware, at a very early age, of the struggle within each of us between good and evil, and the daily crossroads that each of us come across.

I remember one such crossroad in my own life. I was in the seventh grade. Walking home one day from junior high school, I took a short cut through an apartment complex. As I passed by the apartment's mailboxes, I saw a package from a cereal company lying in the tray. No doubt the child who had sent away for the toy was waiting for it with much anticipation. I stood looking at the package, wanting to take it. I remember standing there for what seemed like an eternity, wondering what kind of toy was inside. No one was around. I could have taken the package and nobody would have known, nobody except the child who had saved the box tops and sent away for the toy. But he or she would never have known that I took the toy.

I walked away from the mailbox without the package, but I can still remember to this day how incredibly difficult it was to do what was right. It took me awhile, but finally, at the age of thirty-six, I came to understand why it was so important to me that I always try to do right. My choice for good came in rebellion to my father's dedication of me to evil at the early age of seven; I promised myself I would always try to do good.

After a few sessions trying to put my life into perspective, I spent one counseling session explaining to Dick a spiritual truth I had come to see. When I began therapy, making a commitment to face the ghosts of my past had absolutely terrified me. I felt like a vulnerable child. I was frightened to think what the impact might be as I embraced the pain and memories of my childhood a second time. As I sat in that session reflecting back on my quest for wholeness, I remembered how terrified I had been, feeling as if I was standing on the edge of the valley of the shadow of death.

Once I embarked on my journey it was a lot like childbirth; there was no turning back. I went on to explain that now, after more than three years of counseling, I was on the other side of that valley, looking back in amazement. I could see that it was only a smokescreen. Looking back over the clearing smoke, I could see that I had been deceived, like Eve in the

Garden Of Eden. Instead of being a small vulnerable little child, I was really ten times bigger, ten times smarter, and ten times stronger than that small child. That was the spiritual truth my journey had taught me.

Dick was furiously taking notes as I spoke non-stop. Then he looked up at me and beamed from ear to ear with the smile of a proud parent. "You've made it!" He exclaimed. He went on to say, "Many incest survivors get 'stuck' in the anger, and for a while I worried that you might also." I could understand his concern; I had known some of those people who lived out their lives in anger. But long ago I had seen that waking up every morning and going to bed every night angry at the world was as detrimental as the sins that had been committed against me.

As I sat in Dick's office that day I told him, "I am angry, but not about the physical abuse or Daddy's sadistic reign of terror, not even about the incest. What I'm really angry about is that I bought into a lie, which made me believe that I wouldn't survive embracing the pain of my childhood a second time, a lie that kept me living in reaction to the sins committed against me, caught in a web, unable to free myself."

Soon after that session, Dick started talking about closure. He suggested that we schedule one or two more appointments to wrap things up. He felt like I was well on the road to recovery and going to be fine. I agreed. I was feeling like I needed to get on with my life. It was time to say good-bye.

That week when I sat down to watch television, the Wizard of Oz came on. I began to watch, intrigued. I sat in front of the television set absorbed with the characters and songs. The movie reminded me of my recent journey through my past. Near the beginning of the movie, when Dorothy looked down to see the ruby slippers on her feet, she was told by Glenda the Good Witch of the North, "Keep tight inside of them. Their magic must be powerful or the wicked witch of the west wouldn't want them so badly." Then when Dorothy, the Tinman, and the Scarecrow entered the dark forest, the Scarecrow looked at Dorothy and said, "It gets darker, before it gets lighter." My own journey had been the same.

When they reached their destination, they petitioned the Wizard of Oz: the Scarecrow wanted a brain, the Lion wanted courage, the Tinman wanted a heart and Dorothy wanted to go home. The Wizard of Oz knew they were each in search of something they already had, and he validated that truth to each one of them. To the Scarecrow, the Wizard gave a diploma saying, "By the power vested in me, I now give you this diploma and grant you a Th. D. You are now a Doctor of Thinkology." To the Lion, the Wizard said, "You, my friend, are a victim of disorganized thinking. You have confused courage with wisdom— sometimes it is wise to turn and run." Then the Wizard gave the Lion a medal of courage. To the Tinman, the Wizard gave a testimonial heart then said, "Remember, a heart is not judged by how much you love, but by how much you are loved by others." The Wizard of Oz did not give them anything they did not already have. I knew the search for my heart was the same.

I went to my last appointment with Dick thinking about the role he had played in my recovery, much like the role the Wizard of Oz had played for the Tinman, the Scarecrow, and the Lion. But I also knew that even though he had played an essential part in my recovery, that I was largely responsible for the successful completion of my journey. I, like Dorothy, had kept tight inside of the ruby slippers. I had come to see that I had what it took to make it through that dark valley, even though at the time I entered into it, I felt helpless and afraid.

In Search of My Heart

CHAPTER ELEVEN
THE PROPHECY FULFILLED

Counseling ended with my feeling different about everyday life. For the most part, I was able to accept my childhood losses. My lifelong attitude of "Life's a bitch and then you die" no longer permeated my every thought. My energy was renewed and seemed to be pointed in the direction of finding happiness. This search was constantly on my mind, as if I might pass it by and not notice. I was always on guard and watching for it, like a pot of gold at the end of the rainbow.

The following months were filled with good days and bad days. On the good days when the sadness was held at bay, I was filled with optimism that my search would be successful. The bad days would remind me how life had always been and sometimes overpowered my hope to find happiness. One night as I began to write in my journal, I remembered the statement made to me when I was pregnant with Stephanie, seventeen years before. The words were still as clear as the morning they first entered my mind.

**"In your womb I have planted my seed
and his name shall be called Isaac."**

Those mysterious words still puzzled me. I went to the bookshelf and got the dictionary. I wondered what the name "Isaac" meant. In the back of the dictionary in the listing of names, I found it: Isaac - a Hebrew name meaning "laughter." I sat for a few moments, trying to take in the meaning. Could it be that those words were a promise that one day I would know happiness? That one day I would know laughter and joy? I read in the Bible the account of Abraham and his son Isaac, how God tested the faith of His servant by requiring him to sacrifice his only son. But Abraham remembered God's promise, "I will establish My covenant or solemn pledge with Isaac for an everlasting covenant, and with his posterity after him". And the story goes on to speak of God's goodness; at the very moment when Abraham raised the knife over Isaac, Abraham heard a noise and looked over to see a ram, caught in a thicket. God had provided a sacrifice instead of Isaac! I thought about when I began my journey into what seemed like the valley of death; how scared I was. I wondered if I would survive. Then I realized that I too was required to put my complete faith in God. Maybe the seed that was planted was the seed of faith. Somehow I must have known deep inside that God would also provide a way out for me.

Over the next few months I continued to struggle with sadness. Though my cynicism was fading, I could not completely let it go. After struggling with the lingering sadness, it became evident that I needed some help. Rick was concerned. He wanted me to see a doctor, so I scheduled an appointment with our family physician. Rick went with me. I sat on the table as the Nurse took my temperature and blood pressure. She left the room saying, "The doctor will be in shortly." When the doctor came in, he looked at me and asked, "What's wrong?" I described the life-long symptoms I had lived with: " I just don't feel well. I don't have any energy, I'm always tired. If I could, I'd stay in bed all day." He examined me, then ordered a series of blood tests. He suggested that I schedule a follow-up appointment in one week and said he should have the test results back by then.

The gloom that had always been a part of my life continued. In one week Rick and I returned for the scheduled appointment. The doctor stated, "The results of the blood tests I ordered are all within normal ranges. Everything looks perfectly normal." Then he asked, "What's going on in your life?" I sat there on the examining table and looked at Rick sitting in the chair. The words everything looks perfectly normal kept going through my mind, over and over again. That was the story of my life—everything always looked perfectly normal. I looked at the doctor and said, "The past couple of years have been tough. I've been in counseling, dealing with incest and physical abuse from my childhood." The doctor offered his diagnosis—depression—and gave me a prescription for anti-depressants.

I waited outside for Rick while the prescription was being filled. The sky was filled with dark gray clouds, like my life had always been. I began to cry. When Rick came out and saw that I had been crying, he put his arm around me and said, "Don't worry. Everything will be all right." I wasn't convinced. With all that I had faced and as far as I had come, would I ever get over this sadness? Would I ever be able to say, "Life is good, I'm happy"?

I couldn't face work the next day, so I stayed home. I was puzzled. Why had my search for happiness, embarked on with such vigor, ended in such futility? I stayed in bed all day and read my journals. It felt good to see how far I had come. I called Mother and cried; she always seemed to understand. After talking to Mom, I felt a little better. I crawled back into bed and continued going back through my journals. I read about how the incest survivors' group had ended, with each participant taking responsibility for any role they may have played in the incidents of abuse. I remembered being baffled by this concept. Why would any counselor require the victims of abuse to assume such responsibility?

I spent the next few days pondering the concept of victims taking responsibility for the role they played. One morning I was drinking a cup of coffee, contemplating the issue which made no sense to me, when it dawned on me what my role was! A light bulb went on in my head! That was the key: what I needed to take responsibility for was my attitude about life. Instantly I knew, as if some spiritual truth had been revealed to me, why taking responsibility for the role I played was important. The role I played was what I had the power to change. Taking responsibility for my lifelong attitude of "life's a bitch, then you die" gave me the power to change it. I could choose to see life differently if I really wanted to.

A few days later I received a card in the mail from Mom. Inside she'd written

To Becky;
> In Search of Joy
> I wish you:
>> flowers in your garden
>> coffee in your cup
>> little trills of laughter
>> giggles by the gulp.
>> Tee hees by the trillion
>> chuckles by the score
>> til sides are held
>> and moans are heard
> "Enough, and then some more!"

> Love,
> Mom

Mother always knew when to offer words of encouragement. During the next year I found the depression fading away, each day a little better than the one before. I accepted the reality that I will never be able to recoup my childhood losses. I see my past as always being a part of me, and I know that who I am today is because of what I have been through. My past no longer controls my every move. I'm able to live life now without reacting so much to the pain, with much more understanding and appreciation of who I am. I no longer feel like a victim of circumstance, forced to play out the hand that life dealt me. I've come to see my life as a tapestry woven of rich colors.

One morning that next spring I poured myself a cup of coffee to drink in the warm morning sunlight while admiring my tulip garden. I realized that my mother's wish for me had come true. One evening not long after that, Rick and I were watching one of our favorite television sitcoms when I let out a belly laugh that sounded a little bit like one of Old St. Nick's "Ho! Ho! Ho's!". I looked at Rick startled, and asked him, "Did you hear that? Did you hear me laugh?" I had never heard myself laugh like that before. Then I remembered those prophetic words— Isaac had been born!

Post-Script

The years have been good since the writing of my story. I have not suffered from depression since therapy ended. In case you're wondering; no, I am not taking any medication for depression. I am constantly reminded that my life is no longer filled with pain because my perspective on life has changed. I am more aware now of the good in the world rather than the bad. When I was in counseling I rarely noticed the good in the world, now it's hard for me not to notice it.

Occasionally a good memory from my childhood will surface. Like the other day when Tom Hanks was on Oprah; they were discussing favorite things and he talked about a frosty mug of rootbeer. Their voices faded into the background as I sat on the couch daydreaming. I was remembering a hot summer afternoon in Las Cruces, the scorching desert sun was blazing in the mid-afternoon sky. Papa, my sisters and I were sitting in Papa's car under the shade of the A&W root beer stand. The car windows were down and the hot summer air was blowing across our skin. We were laughing and talking as we sipped on the frosty mugs of ice-cold A & W root beer. The quenching sweetness of the ice cold brew was sooooo good!

But it would not be true to say that all my days are full of joy. In fact, I still struggle with coming into living a really joyful existence. I am not sure how realistic that kind of existence is. In my struggle, I have come to understand why it is difficult for me to let my guard down and play; because when I was little that's when the enemy attacked. So now I am in the process of trying to figure out a way to reprogram myself. I have contemplated lately the thought of anointing myself with the oil of joy and then having a movie marathon with the three stooges. My only hesitation is that I may become someone that is so full of joy, someone that laughs at everything and anything, someone so obnoxious, that no one will want to be around me. So if you meet me in the future and I appear to be hysterically happy, believe me when I tell you that the oil of joy and the three stooges movie marathon was effective.

Becky

Order Information

To obtain order information for a recording of 'Lord of the Past' write to the address listed below or direct an inquiry to Bob Bennett at his e-mail address: brightav@ix.netcom.com

Bright Avenue Songs
P.O. Box 1578
Cypress, CA 90630-6578

publishing company

Words of HOPE Publishing Company
P O Box 10597
Albuquerque, NM   87184-0597
Phone: (505) 792-4490
Fax: (505) 792-4491
email: info@wordsofhope.com

Title	Quantity Ordered	Price
In Search of My Heart @ $ 16.95		$
	Shipping & Handling @ $ 3.00	$
	Subtotal	$
	State Tax (If ordering in New Mexico) 5.375%	$
	Total	$

METHOD OF PAYMENT:

☐ Check OR Money Order Enclosed (payable to Words of HOPE Publishing Co.)

☐ Visa   ☐ Mastercard   ☐ American Express   ☐ Discover
Expiration Date: Month   ☐☐   Year   ☐☐

Name of Card Holder (Please Print): _____

Signature of Card Holder _____

CARD NUMBER: ☐☐☐☐☐☐☐☐☐☐☐☐☐☐☐☐

SHIP TO:

NAME: _____

ADDRESS: _____

CITY: _____

STATE: _____   ZIP: _____

PHONE: (   )   -

Please provide phone in case of questions

COPY THIS PAGE AND USE IT AS YOUR ORDER FORM. THEN MAIL OR FAX IT TO US.

In Search of My Heart